This book is a gift from
Susan S. Williams
in loving memory of her mother,
Lodema D. Somers

busy baby animals

elephant

Please visit our web site at: www.garethstevens.com
For a free color catalog describing Gareth Stevens' list of high-quality books
and multimedia programs, call 1-800-542-2595 (USA) or 1-800-461-9120 (Canada).
Gareth Stevens Publishing's Fax: (414) 332-3567.

Library of Congress Cataloging-in-Publication Data

Johnson, Jinny.
    Elephant / by Jinny Johnson; [illustrated by Ch'en-Ling; photography by Simon Murrell].
    —North American ed.
        p. cm. — (Busy baby animals)
    ISBN 0-8368-2923-9 (lib. bdg.)
    1. Elephants—Infancy—Juvenile literature. [1. Elephants. 2. Animals—Infancy.]
I. Ch'en-Ling, ill. II. Murrell, Simon, ill. III. Title.
QL737.P98J617   2001
599.67'139—dc21   2001020532

This North American edition first published in 2001 by
Gareth Stevens Publishing
A World Almanac Education Group Company
330 West Olive Street, Suite 100
Milwaukee, Wisconsin 53212 USA

This U.S. edition © 2001 by Gareth Stevens, Inc. Original edition © 1999 by
Marshall Editions Developments Ltd. First published in 1999 by Marshall
Publishing Ltd., London, England.

Illustrations: Ch'en-Ling
Photography: Simon Murrell, Animal Ark
Editor: Sadie Smith
Designer: Siân Williams
Gareth Stevens editor: Katherine J. Meitner
Gareth Stevens cover design: Katherine A. Kroll

Printed in the United States of America

1 2 3 4 5 6 7 8 9 05 04 03 02 01

busy baby animals

elephant

Jinny Johnson

Gareth Stevens Publishing

A WORLD ALMANAC EDUCATION GROUP COMPANY

Noorie is an Asian elephant. She lives on the grasslands in a herd with her mother and aunts and lots of cousins.

Look at Noorie's long trunk. She uses it to drink. Noorie sucks water into her trunk. Then she squirts the water into her mouth.

Noorie uses her trunk to do lots of things. She can smell with it. She can also say hello to other elephants by touching them with it.

Baby elephants love to play. Noorie and her friends like to chase each other. Look, Noorie has found a log to play with.

11

Young elephants have a lot to learn. Noorie's mother shows her where to find food and water. She also teaches her how to stay safe.

Grown elephants sleep standing up. But Noorie usually lies down in a shady spot on the ground. Sleep well, Noorie.

14

More about Elephants

Elephants live in the forests and grasslands of Africa and Asia. Elephant families are usually made up of related females and their young. The leader of the herd is often the oldest or biggest elephant. Mother elephants, as well as other females in the herd, care for the baby elephants, called calves. Calves drink their mother's milk for two or more years, but they also start to eat leaves and grass when they are three months old. When they grow up, females stay with the herd. Males leave, when they are about twelve years old, to wander alone or with other males.